CASE WORKER LIED

(leading to a winning lawsuit decision in 3ʳᵈ Cir;)

"Who chose malfeasance/wrongful acts over doing what was right for two little girls and a great parent, who now have WON such right to see their MULTI- MILLION, in damages move forward without a lawyer known as pro-se(self file) against abhorrent Child Protection Services state DCF employee, holding such per state employee accountable, one discovery at at a time, by deadline."

I0511226

Author:

Women **4 JUSTICE** Publishing N.Y.C.

in association with:

T.A.N .

(TAKE **ACTION** NETWORK.)

+

POWERHOUSE WOMEN

#LEARN #ACHIEVE and #WIN

<u>PREFACE-INTRODUCTION</u>

A dystopian tale, a true-story where a state employee has left a child in direct harms way, then expected to walk away scott free, with such agency backing her, until the suit was taken to a U.S. District FEDERAL Magistrate. Such parochial caseworker assumed it would just all go away. The small-minded nefarious, the bad soul she and he are, all assumed wrong. This time? They have met the wrong parent,as expert cite to the author for years.

For a long time:

I've met good caseworker/social workers who really are into the protecting of a child who has been harmed, and really was abused, where the evidence support such fact and the caseworker is making sure in a court of law the TRUTH is told/FACTS are presented without alteration of such facts,misrepresentation,excluding perjury, no fraud.

However, such books are focusing NOT on the good souls who are every day they awake are focus on helping kids in dire need of being rescued.

This author, her children were not in any need on July 3rd 4th weekend to be "rescued." The rescuing came "after" the children, healthy alert happy un-abused, were dropped off at a weekend visit (per court order)with dad at his mom's house for a visit on Friday to be returned on a Sunday at approximately 7:p.m. Hours...Days would go by, as I, a good parent simply had to wait, and wait...and wait...

CHAPTER I-

The events remain on the author's mind indefinite.

Caseworker is now being held accountable and or plural "caseworker's, state employees."

The bias *state court* at the time, allowed for such farce of a case to stand. But this is not how it is in the U.S. District **FEDERAL** Court. Best thing about the Federal court is the judge is really hearing and seeing "what has happened, involving such employees at child protection services, and not turning a blind-eye."

Chapter II-

When a caseworker for child protection services,

CYS,ACS,CHFS,DFPS,DCFS,DFS,DYFS,DHS,DSS elect to hinder, rather than to disclose such truth involving a family and or a loving parent/grandparent/children et.al.,

so many children across our nation shall continue to suffer great harm.

Recently in NEW YORK CITY, FLORIDA,TENNESSEE,few other states down south and north and toward west have been arrested for falsified information knowingly given to a judge, to perjury,and this is a wonderful thing to see.

It gives others, still violated so much hope as such inequities, violations,wrongful acts by caseworker is ubiquitous, and not in any way non-prevalent.

When a caseworker is sworn to tell the truth,but yet knowingly have altered evidence/lied/falsified and provided consistent false and knowingly false statements, hinder evidence, while manufacturing the events prior to court, there is no justice for America's **_most_** beautiful and that is the innocence of a once pure happy, little girl, or boy who has been taken into state custody, known as a "seizure,hence in violation of the clearly established-

fourth,and or one's fourteenth amendment of the United States Constitution."

Each and every incident report that were made against

the abusive step-mother of the author girls and the troubled ex spouse(a known serious convicted felon, who served prison/jail time,and a known heroine distributor-heroine user for years since his teenage years,and crack-cocaine caucasian alcoholic) each allegation made about both troubled abusive individuals, were seemingly deemed false.Always were deemed as un-substantiated and not established/Un-founded.

A jury shall know this as well as other relevant facts pointing to an agenda, as the motive was clear when you're building the mental visual, and you're doing so with substantial significant evidence everyone.

The caseworkers, during such time, in the prior FN matter(Family SUPERIOR Court Family neglect case)for some time have repeatedly failed to turn over:

1.) CPS social worker dcf visit(s)each week with the child to check on both girls well-being while out of the mothers primary care/custody, as required by law,as this for the first not 1 but 5 yrs was not done,for almost six years actually.Only sporatic.

2.) Even the sporatic visit-intake log demonstrate a devoid of implementation of the actual DYFS cps worker(child protection services worker's sheets, that are supposed to be legible,clear format,readable and signed with such truthfulness/facts et.al.,)

3.) Medical reports, DENTAL reports, SCHOOL reports from age 7 years old NOT seen anywhere,and age 10, in the defendants file/internal caseworker notes,and or teacher reports, updates et.al., entire time the girls were in the Division Youth Family Services/Division Child Protection & Permanency, the Department Children and Families file, as such discovery now prove.

Such plaintiff when suing has properly pled throughout that moreover, the Defendants, herein; refer to as the "DEFTS" at Division Child Protection & Permanency herein; "CPP or "DYFS or "DCF" or DCPP" were OBLIGATED by statutes internal dcf agency cps policies, regulations, et.al., to visit and also to moreover inspect the living conditions, of both of the children, belonging to the owner.

CHAPTER III

 What the defense failed to expound (still) many years later everyone)as a jury shall see, when granted the right to move forward through SUMMARY JUDGEMENT/MTD(motion to dismiss) is why when a child was visiting on a weekend visit, a non-custodial parent residence/grandparent house,in Plainfield,NJ who was already proven healthy,ALERT

and as the police dept., and defendant J.L.H..,

 cite on day in question and weekend in question,

 "Child *is fine*."

No need to go and talk with the mother.

As the ten year old very young child and her little sister, only 7 were being stuck at a house that was NOT their comfort-zone, their home,with mom, the agency worker's, rather than focus on doing what is right by focusing on children who are abused and at risk each day, the worker's were conspiring to deprive a good hard-working astute loving parent of her rights.

While the girls were seized, under state supervision after multi-policemen, and a caseworker J.L.H.(listed in the publicized suit) were all in agreement, "No substantiated abuse/no neglect to the girls, and how the girls can go home, the state worker(s)were still attempting to and indeed, violated the daughter rights as her younger sister and the mom's as the record will show, to a jury of their peers,for damages is they survive summary judgement phase.

Chapter IV-

Cops and a DYFS(dcf/dcpp employee, did not even need to go see mom at home,and or call mom,since after all there was simply NO ABUSE/NO IMMINENT DANGER, and no neglect at all substantiated)

This part must be underscore to all of our readers around the world that:

You're having first a police dept.,and a DYFS cps employee at almost midnight weekend of a holiday July 3rd/4th in the 2000's advising and discussing while child is there, how despite what was reported by first an "anonymous caller, then the grandmother name was exerted, the police and a state employee are clearly in agreement and citing "after investigating and after they met with the very young child, all agreed, no abuse,and no medical attention needed, said by dyfs and the police,and how there was just "no reason"to go speak to mom, the child is fine and there is no substantiated of abuse and or not even neglect. "Child is fine." No need to go and talk with the mother.

T hat is <u>proof</u> right there to any reasonable jury, the child was not, at what is known as <u>IMMINENT RISK.</u>

CASEWORKER AGAIN CLEARED MOM 1st time july3rd/4th and went home after going to the police dept., to investigate with the police.

Chapter V-

July 5th-through July 9th there were at least 2 more workers now who were called in to also investigate, but keep in mind everyone, as the jury shall be reminded of by the injured parties and lawyer that(through 1-through 7 are significant for the child 4th amendment constitutional right claim,clearly established.)

1. July 5th S.A.(Defendant) also said how there was no abuse, and how on July 9th (only after mom called abuse hotline @ DYFS to report that her children are still over grandmother house(father's troubled mother residence) and they have not been returned when mom has clearly full legal SOLE custody since her divorce from such junkie addict K.S.)

2. The worker *__finally__* arrived on July 9th, finally,after 1 week, she arrive to talk with mom.(Bonafide violation as all experts agree nationwide.) The girls are stuck at a home **NOT** theirs, no 1 tells mom at all and now finally (only because mom call the agency after talking to the police dept; is there now a worker finally "getting around to interviewing mom on the evening of July 9th

8

almost July 10th as the clock was heading toward 11:30 or so to 11:45 p.m.) and the worker looked all through the house, et.al.,

and went over the "july 3rd/4th allegation of a spanking that resulted in "serious injuries and so that was her basis to being at my residence."

3. After the caseworker G.C.W. seen the parent's 1 family BI-LEVEL house with a pool in the back, the author girls wood-oak-pink Barbie theme-bedroom and an extra TOY-ROOM right next door for the girls to play in with so many toys for each child, and clothing,shoes, and books for learning, nestled on a suburban area residential quiet tree-lined street.

4. Walking out with the mother, the caseworker, now lawsuit defendant G.C.W. cites, I have to APOLOGIZE on behalf of UNION COUNTY,NJ DIVISION.(dyfs) as this is not how we "usually conduct our business as a caseworker."I have to apologize. You should have been contacted from day ONE over a week ago, and your kids are still there? You're allowed to go and get your girls, right now. I don't see ANY reason as to WHY you can't bring your girls back home. DYFS *can't* substantiate child abuse, or neglect.

5. Parents spank their children and I didn't see any serious injuries, rising ***to the level needed*** to keep a child away from its parent, none at all. I examine her,before meeting you, and I seen the younger sibling too.I will also add this all to my report.

9

6. You are allowed to go and pick up your children.

   Author said, due to the lateness of the hour, I would let them sleep,(looked at clock again and now it was well after 12:45 a.m.)and the caseworker agreed, OK. Pick them up in the morning and just "follow up" with the division and we also will reach out too again in the near future.

   Worker re-iterated she had to "apologize because this is just not how DYFS ever conduct business,and even brought up about how the girls were clearly well taken care of, as their home."

7. I will call and advise the PGM, that you're going to get your girls.DYFS can'ts substantiate abuse against you or even neglect. Mom was so happy after not holding'seeing her girls for 1 week. This part right here is huge,and shall be significant to any reasonable-minded juror reading/seeing the truth/going over evidence from this day and prior week july 3rd 4th weekend, everyone.

8. Another report surfaced giving even more credence to the cementing of the child's 4th amendment claim for damages and that is, another worker "even after state agency caseworker later altered her reports/record et.al., in violation of law,and the family rights, the worker initial S.A., spoke during week of july 9th – 15th had spoke again to another office, this time a detective.

9. The same exact day this was told to another policemen the state agency were in court!(the record reflect such factual)and or within 24 hours of the O.T.S.C..(order to show cause)as to why the girls should "remain" in state

custody, "after" being in state custody 2 weeks prior without the NECESSARY JUDICIAL COURT ORDER and or a warrant to keep the girls.

10. S.A. informed the police detective that the child yes, has been removed and that "The child is with the PGM, **HOWEVER**, NJ DYFS can't substantiate <mark>ANY</mark> abuse assault complaint against the mother." [End Quote]

 JURY SHALL HAVE THIS IN THEIR

POSSESSION in 2017. A JURY will have the opportunity to HEAR the mother and the child tell their truthful story insofar as what happened.

The jury will know once again during the entire almost 2 weeks of a child, a little girl being seize as her younger sister, you had caseworker's rather than PROTECTING a really abused child were gearing up to commit fraud on the court/malfeasance for years to come.

As a result, the child suffered and mom gravely, for almost a decade.

Chapter VI-

Contrary to what lies and daily court hearings fabrication by the state worker's this is how the law works when you're aggressively and steadfast, focus and learning the law inside out when it comes to procedural involving a state employee so be sure to continue to learn as much as feasible when you're at the point of exercising your constitutional rights and fundamental right and your civil rights, as a family at each state level and when you're reading our books, docu-series we are sure many of you in the world are able to relate to what the author has been through, and why her mission as her family is so clear insofar as fighting for what is RIGHT and that is not only justice but clear accountability and FINAL JUSTICE in which experts agree, is a "long time coming for this once happy suburban good family."

Despite a caseworker attempting and thinly-argued by a "D.A.G." representing the defendant, it is <u>not</u> in any unclear.

You can't keep a child away from going home, in other words as our other federal courts,and our third circuit (NJ-DE-PA)3rd Cir; to NINTH CIRCUIT;(California) cite clearly, "Absent Imminent Danger/Exigent Circumstances, a child has a right to go home,and not continued to be **SEIZE**, in violation of his or her *<u>well-established 4th</u>* amendment." It really is *as simple* as that.

CHAPTER VII-

The New Jersey Child Protection Agency "DCPP" and "DCF/DYFS" without any court authorization, took a child into state custody, known as a seizure,for a whole 13 to 14 days.Child also is suing for the fact a worker failed to allow her mother to have a court date scheduled within the first 24-48 or 72 hours after child was taken into state custody with a court order,without imminent danger, that led to the child having to languish and remain out of her own home, that much longer, when she was supposed to be return and allow to go home,since no abuse was substantiated. When such worker did such as other state employees, mom had no clue what was going on, until a week later when she finally was informed by a policemen, to call the DYFS agency in Union County, as they are the ones who took the child, even though the child was **not** injured nor abused, and the officer then went over more with author on how the caseworker, indeed was there when the police and DYFS both agreed to such fact.

State attorney representing such liable defendants cite how "the DODD removal allow the worker's to take the child."However, he is mistaken in this case and a jury shall agree premise on:

1. A DODD NJ removal of a child is only for 2 things.

2. Removing a child premise on "imminent danger and or exigency circumstances that has arise to where there wouldn't have been enough time, to procure a judge authorization, everyone.

➤ Let's now look **at the time frame**, supporting child's 4th amendment claim for damages associated with her removal for almost 8 inexcusable years.

➤ Child is dropped off early morning everyone. Approximate time was 9:a.m. or so in the morning, to the grandmother's to see dad for his usual court-ordered weekend july 4th weekend.

➤ The police report does not show any involvement until 12 hours, "after" drop-off to grandmother's residence. Yes everyone, you read it right. 12 hours LATER.

➤ This...right here is crucial relating to whether or not the state agency/individual worker's had "enough time, to procure the necessary warrant and or a judicial "emergent-authorization from a judge, to seize such child, take them into state custody." THIS WAS NOT DONE.

Next ...

After July 4th ... You're now looking at July 7th(Monday) morning. The defendant(s) S.A., J.H., and supervisor at the time caseworker C.N., all still have not at this time gone to court and or make a simple call to procure the authorization to seize such child/take her into state custody with her sister AS REQUIRED; when

    a.) No imminent danger is clearly the issue.

    b.) No serious injuries/no serious harm to child at "that very moment, everyone."

    c.) No exigent circumstances whatsoever.

Let us count the days that the state workers, again supporting a 4th amendment violation/damages/claim for the child.

    1.) July 5th -still no warrant/judicial court authorization.

    2.) July 6th, July 7th, July 8th, July 9th, July 10th,July 11th.

    3.) July 12th July 13th, July 14th, July 15th... It took the state defendants ALMOST 2 full weeks from July 3rd (The day the kids were healthy/alert/happy and un-abused, from july 3rd- throughout July 15th or 16th NO COURT ORDER/NO WARRANT to keep the girls away from returning home knowing there were no serious injuries,

15

rising to level of what is considered as "imminent" as all case law wholly support. The state worker had <u>enough time</u> to procure the actual court order judicial authorization, but chose not to. This is fact. .Not a fictional account/not conjecture. Not bald assertion, not a falsity but 100% factual.

The state workers conspired to violate a child right in the state of New Jersey by:

➤ Ignoring their own statute/policies et.al.,

➤ Ignoring their own documentation!

➤ Ignoring their own written reports that there was NO SUBSTANTIATION OF ABUSE.

➤ Ignoring their own state policies,federal et.al, as to such law that allow a child in the state of NJ to simply return home, when a child, at the time is not at IMMINENT RISK, on the day in question.

Let us make a crucial note here, while going into the relevant phase of SUMMARY JUDGEMENT everyone.

" The child, even if the state D.A.G. representing the liable caseworker, tries to invoked, and we have no doubt he will to save their neck, from clear act(s) of wrongful acts/bad faith/intentionally/knowingly et.al., able to be proven, but let's just say for arguemen sake, when the lawyer attempt to say,

"Well, the girls were at imminent risk of danger on the day of July 3rd, premise on she was allegedly to have been spank,hit known as "excessive" corporal.

Even if, for argument sake, as a jury shall hear the child was disciplined on or about july 3rd weekend.

So…

 what is their excuse for :

1. <u>Not </u>speaking to the mother,who is allegedly the one who seriously harmed her own child til' <u>7 whole days or so later.</u>

2. Not at any time, procuring the <u>NECESSARY</u> warrant of removal through court ordered judicial authorization after July 3rd 4th after the weekend, when "Court was OPEN on Monday July 6th-July 7th.

3. Then the second week of keeping the girls, BOTH for another week almost, in totality 2 weeks throughout July 15th 16th.

4. There couldn't have been "imminent danger going back to the 3rd or 4th since such facts support there was no imminent risk i.e., but not limited to:

   A.) Child was already seen by the police july 3rd

   B.) Child was already seen by a dyfs employee(s).

   C.) Child was said to have been alert, happy,f ine.

   D.) Cop cite, "No medical attention required and the child is fine, can go home. DYFS agreed.

   E.) DYFS & cop agree, "Child has left the police dept, and is fine,no abuse, **_so no need_** to go and see/speak to the mother at her home that night.No need."

   F.) DYFS worker "allegedly"procure a dr.report.

G.) But yet, the dr. report was clearly written by multiple other parties,and not only the dr., and or as an ==expert cites==, "not by a dr., at all,as the penmanship/writing was clearly copies done over by multiple other parties.

H.) Even with the dr.report "allegedly taken on july 4th, by an un-qualified physician who later admit to mom that she was *not* "trained in the field of suspected abuse" and or neglect.

And again, let's say for argument sake this feign-fake dr.,report was real, it still did not,at any time support any serious injuries rising to the level of imminent danger/exigent circumstance, OR the state defendants, by law would have immediately had to, without further delay:

➢ Take the child into state custody without a court order, AND such entitle the parent accused to a quick 24hr.to 72hour court hearing in front of a **judge, in family superior court.**

➢ *Advise the local union county prosecutor immediate without delay.None of what you're reading was ever done. Prosecutor, through this day, still validate.*

All of what is being enumerated in our book series Volume 1 through 15 and this new book are in support of the child's American Civil Rights, in support of the child's significant 4th amendment violation claim.

What was done was all that was wrong including but not limited to:

> ➤ ALTERED MEDICAL RECORD to support "trauma and serious injuries on an un-injure child."

> ➤ ALTERED FILE INTERNAL CPS RECORD by a liable caseworker who knew (prior to such alteration) the child was allowed, as caseworker cite in clear English,to return home.

> ➤ Evidence of such exculpatory nature clearly withheld,knowingly by at least 2 or 3 defendants.

> ➤ Caseworkers, knew for years the father had such a strong propensity to cause great harm being a drug addict/alcoholic to both girls **if ever given a chance at custody, let alone sole legal full custody**, and to make all medical legal decisions, but yet allowed and advocated for a junkie unfit person to procure custody after all of the wrongful act(s)illegal and unconstitutional actions of the workers for which has clearly harmed a child for

almost 8 years without her mother affection,nurture, love as she she has received for the first long 10 years of her very young life.

- ➢ DCF simply just let the kids stay in a house that was not their own, with people who are known to use drugs, crack-cocaine/heroine/injecting heroine since his teen years, already on the record everyone.

Stay tuned…

More to come…

This now shall conclude another book, part of our docu-series being implemented involving such multi-million dollar civil rights lawsuit against not one,but several workers who knew what to do, and chose to commit the complete anti-thesis,(The complete opposite) in violation of her right, as well as the author's own civil rights

This all that is featured in this book, shall support the child's civil rights 4th amendment claim, in accordance to our United States Constitution.

By the time the investigation was taken place on July 3rd and July 4th the police had again earlier already determined that there was <u>no evidence</u> of wrongdoing/injuries rising to any level of child abuse and or even neglect. DYFS knew.

A jury question shall be as experts and case law support:

Was at anytime a caseworker, within such possession and knowledge that there was:

1. A report citing, "mom is able to get the kids.

2. A report citing and or that "DYFS worker cannot PROVE/SUBSTANTIATE abuse

3. DYFS DCF "has investigated and we have(we)referring to DYFS has no LEGAL RIGHT, and or NO LEGAL AUTHORITY to KEEP THE GIRLS FROM GOING HOME to their mom,since no abuse was even substantiated by such defendant(s).

4. Was the child on the day in question on either July 3rd and or July 4th and or ANY

time on the weekend throughout July 5th at imminent danger,or is it true a COP, actually several and severa CPS employees all agree, "child is fine and healthy,alert,hence no need to keep child out of the mother's home, and certainly without the NECESSARY JUDICIAL AUTHORIZATION/COURT ORDER from such time after the weekend for almost 14 days."

JURY shall be presented after summary judgement with such mandatory and most relevant queries by author's plaintiff law team.

Remember everyone:

5. DYFS agreed with the police dept., findings and was at the police dept. while such was discussed.

The daughter, still at the father's mother residence had no way to naturally know what was going on. She and her little sister, were planning on continuing to live a life of a CHILD and that was to be safe @ home, not abused, @ home, play at the park, go shopping with mom, be IN school, and have a healthy fun summer filled with fun and the pool in the back of their yard along with going to a carnival, watching blue clues, nickelodeon and other tv modeling auditions with their mother, a model and a NYC recording artist aspiring actress for a long time, since the mother teen years and her daughter's love doing such, with their mom in NY. Now, the daughters, **are at the age to sue** and are doing just that, with their mother. Old enough to face all of their abuser's, the **REAL** abuser's in federal court, 1 by 1 holding them all accountable in a court of law, finally since age of only seven and 10, while smiling knowing that 1 day FINAL JUSTICE shall be visible for others to continue to learn from, and gain perspective from when dealing with a caseworker engaging in the worse crime you're able to take part in, and that is hurting intentionally a child, innocent good parent, and a child who, whereas;

if the caseworker had done what was right, by law, would have not been severely injured not for a day, or week but almost an entire decade. No compensation $$$ can remove the darken scar for a mother loving doting innocent and god-loving, or her girls,

but sure would help others who are somewhere right now,still S.I.T.S.(stuck in the system) and thinking there is no "hope."

The author's suit and org.biz now help others realize even with 1 per **requested 1-on-1 POWER** session assist such person into realizing immediately that you DO have the knowledge, within you.

You do have the POWER in you, to achieve what you're working toward achieving and that is to receive FINAL justice when injured by a state employee.

#YOU<u>ARE</u>CAPABLE

#NEVERGIVEUPThere will be no caseworker anymore, to force either child to lie on their own loving good focus astute doting mother. We are in the FEDERAL court now. And the girls are older, no more to be used as pawns.

There will be no abusive father, nor abusive step-parent to force the girls out of the house/to hurt them anymore, along with <u>DYFS hindering such fact.</u>

There will be no more bias state care(family court) to ignore such clear acts of cps worker,caseworker wrongful acts. Federal Court has spoken.

The rest is history. We shall keep you all posted, when calling our consulting 1-on-1 hep-hotline,and we thank you all for your support, here at the WOMEN 4 JUSTICE PUBLISHING N.Y.C., + #TAN and we pray for you as we know there is some 1 out here right now reading and saying, "This is **similar** to what happen to me."

Ergo, if we can help 1 person, violated by a state employee, and to **prevent** another one from being violated, and or those suing pro-se without a lawyer as our astute author has done, all on her own through the most befuddled,difficult circumstances acting as pro-se, then we know our job is done.

1-929-277-7848   Copyright Protection
2012-2017-2018

THE TIME IS **_ALWAYS_** RIGHT …

TO DO **_WHAT IS RIGHT_** M L K J R .

OUR LIVES BEGIN TO END
THE DAY WE BECOME
SILENT ABOUT
THINGS THAT MATTER.

Martin Luther King Jr.

www.ingramcontent.com/pod-product-compliance
Lightning Source LLC
Chambersburg PA
CBHW041616180526
45159CB00002BC/890